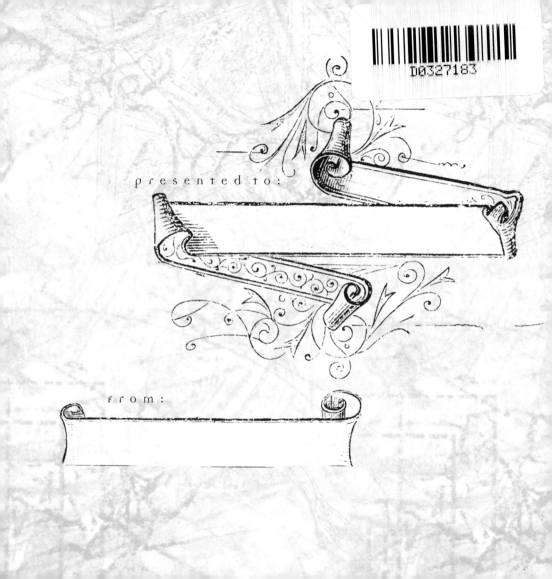

presented to:

from:

WORSHIP

Michael W. Smith

with Wendy Lee Nentwig

J. COUNTRYMAN

NASHVILLE, TENNESSEE

Published by J. Countryman®, a division of Thomas Nelson, Inc.,
Nashville, Tennessee 37214

Project Editor: Kathy Baker

Design: Christopher Gilbert, UDG | DesignWorks

Acknowledgements: "In Touch with the Eternal" and "A Foretaste of Forever." Adapted from It's Time to Be Bold, by Michael W. Smith.
 © 1997. Published by W Publishing.
"Celebrating the Creator." Adapted from This is Your Time, by Michael W. Smith. ©2000. Published by Thomas Nelson, Inc.

ISBN 0-8499-9593-0

Printed and bound in the United States of America

www.thomasnelson.com

A NOTE about the BOOK

Worship is a vital part of our faith. As we recognize god for who He is, we are drawn into a closer relationship with our Father. Our strength is renewed. Our souls are refreshed. With that in mind, we pray that this collection of thoughts on worship will draw you closer to the Creator and lead you to a deeper level of worship in your own life.

I have been a worship leader for more than twenty years, getting my start in 1980 at Belmont Church in my adopted hometown of Nashville, Tennessee, and continuing in that role at my new church, New River Fellowship. Over the years, I've also written my share of worship songs—among them "Agnus Dei," "Great is the Lord," and "Thy Word"—songs that have been sung both by large groups here in America and by small groups meeting secretly on the other side of the world.

I've had many incredible worship experiences, but I am continually reminded that I have not arrived. No matter how much I have witnessed, God always has more in store. And lately something has been happening that I've never been a part of before. I've never seen the power of the Holy Spirit sweep across a generation like I'm seeing today. I'm seeing it closer to home as well. At our little church, we've reached some levels of worship recently that I have never been to in my life, and I have to say, it has just about knocked me out. I'm not naïve enough to think this has anything to do with me. God just showed up.

It happens every day.

When His people cry out to Him with pure hearts, when they sing joyfully about His goodness and grace, when they sit quietly and wait to hear from Him in the midst of their busy day, God shows up. And why wouldn't He? Like all fathers, He delights in spending time with His children.

So I pray that as you read this book, the stories, songs, scripture, and quotations contained within will remind you that we serve a God who is infinitely worthy of all our praise and that they will inspire you to worship Him in spirit and in truth.

MICHAEL W. SMITH

Worship is a lifestyle, but I think that amid all the praise music and worship services it's easy to lose sight of that. I'm very thankful for what's going on now. There are all these new praise and worship songs coming out, expressing what we want to say, which is wonderful. It lifts our spirits and gives us a chance to tell the Lord how we really feel about Him. But music is just a small part of it.

When we go to the checkout counter at the grocery store, how do we treat that person? Reaching out can also be worship, even if it's just the simple act of saying "hello" and offering someone a smile.

The beauty of the gospel is its simplicity. It's "love the Lord your God with all your heart, mind, and strength, and love your neighbor as yourself." That's worship.

Give unto the Lord the glory due to His name;
Worship the Lord in the beauty of holiness.

Psalm 29:2

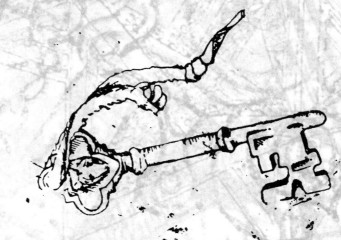

Take my life and let it be

consecrated, Lord, to Thee;

Take my moments and my days,

Let them flow in ceaseless praise.

From the hymn "Take My Life and Let It Be"

Frances R. Havergal (1874)

worship is making time for god.

O ften late in the evening, when the kids are in bed and the phone has stopped ringing, I'll get away for a walk along the road that leads to my house. Or sometimes, early in the morning, before the insanity of my daily schedule kicks in, I'll get in my car and drive through the countryside. These are the times that I seriously connect with God, telling Him everything that's on my heart, or maybe just being still and knowing that He's there.

Worship is celebrating God's provision.

After the parting of the Red Sea, God's people gave credit where it was due.

Then Moses and the children of Israel sang this song to the LORD, and spoke, saying:

"I will sing to the LORD,
for He has triumphed gloriously!
The horse and its rider
He has thrown into the sea!
The LORD *is* my strength and song,
And He has become my salvation;
He *is* my god, and I will praise Him;
My father's god, and I will exalt Him.

EXODUS 15:1-2

The Power of a Song

Those early days at Belmont were a huge influence on me. I'd walk in and have all this baggage, and then a song would just nail me. Through the music, I would be reminded once again how much I desperately needed God in my life.

Certain songs just seem able to do that, as if they have an anointing on them. "Above All," which is one of my favorites, is one of those songs. I sang it for President George W. Bush at his Presidential Inaugural Prayer Service held at Washington National Cathedral in our nation's capital. The tune, written by Lenny LeBlanc and Paul Baloche, had only come to my attention two weeks earlier, when I stumbled across it on a compilation CD. I knew immediately that it was the perfect song to sing for the president. Some songs just seem to have the special hand of God on them.

Worship is what we were created to do.

For we who worship God in the spirit ... put no confidence in human effort. Instead we boast about what Christ Jesus has done for us

Philippians 3:3 NLT

He speaks, and the sound of His voice Is so sweet the birds hush their singing,

And He walks with me, and He talks with me,

   And He tells me I am His own;

And the joy we share as we tarry there,

   None other has ever known.

He speaks, and the sound of His voice

   Is so sweet the birds hush their singing,

And the melody that He gave to me

   Within my heart is ringing.

FROM THE HYMN "IN THE GARDEN"

C. AUSTIN MILES (1913)

worship is giving back to god what is already HIS.

Dear God,

Help us to remember that all good gifts come
from you. Anything we have is merely on loan
to us, and you are waiting patiently for us to
loosen our grip on our meager little treasures
and offer them back to you.

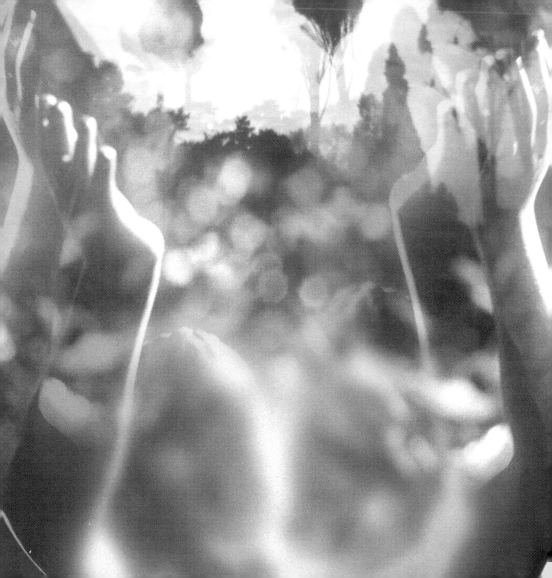

Most High, all-powerful, all good, Lord!

All praise is yours, all glory, all honor

And all blessing.

To you alone, Most High, do they belong.

No mortal lips are worthy

To pronounce your name.

All praise be yours, my Lord, through all that you have made.

. . .praise and bless my Lord, and give Him thanks,

And serve Him with great humility.

from "The Canticle of Brother Sun"

St. Francis of Assisi (1225)

Worship
is a response.

I will praise the Lord at all times.

I will constantly speak of His praises.

I will boast only in the Lord;

Let all who are discouraged take heart.

come, let us tell of the Lord's greatness;

Let us exalt His name together.

psalm 34:1-3 nlt

Praise Amid Pain

It's one thing to praise God when all is going well. You have enough to eat, a roof over your head, work to occupy your hands, and family and friends to share it with. But what about when hard times come and the world is watching to see how you respond?

Job had just received word that his children and all his livestock were dead. Upon hearing the news, the Bible tells us he tore his robe and fell on the ground before God. A fitting response, many would agree. But then he did something unusual: Rather than asking "why me?" as so many of us would do, Job said, "I came naked from my mother's womb, and I will be stripped of everything when I die. The LORD gave me everything I had, and the LORD has taken it away. Praise the name of the LORD!" (Job 1:21, NLT).

There can be a release and a real freedom in worshiping in the hard times. It can be hard to do sometimes, but it works. And through it, God does something to your heart. Things might continue to be tough for a while, but the burden suddenly doesn't feel so heavy. And I think that's just what we're supposed to do. We're supposed to praise Him no matter what.

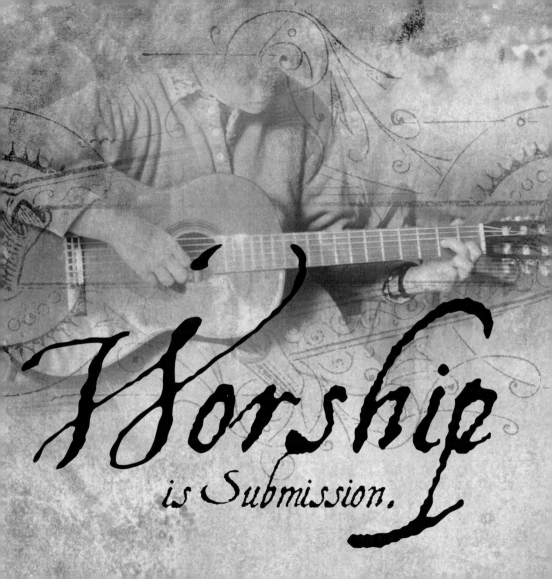

True worship comes in when you let go of the things that have a hold on you and just go, "Lord, this is my life and all this other stuff doesn't mean anything." You let God take control and then suddenly all you want your life to be about is building the kingdom of God. When you get to that place, I can't imagine worship being any better than that.

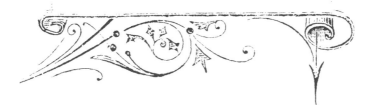

O, worship the King, all glorious above;

O gratefully sing His power and His love;

Our Shield and Defender, the Ancient of Days,

Pavilioned in splendor and girded with praise!

from the hymn "o, worship the king"

robert grant (1833)

34

I t was late, around midnight, or so we're told in Acts 16:25. Paul and Silas found themselves alone, in a dark prison, and facing an uncertain future. Lesser men might have been worrying about what would happen next or wondering if God had forgotten them. But not this faithful twosome.

Although separated from everyone they loved and stripped of their freedom, Paul and Silas kept praying and singing to God, worshiping instead of despairing. Their fellow prisoners noticed their behavior—and they certainly noticed the surprising events that followed. As songs of faith wafted through the jail, an earthquake rocked the place. The cell doors flew open and the prisoners' chains fell away.

Can you imagine what the other prisoners must have thought? We know how the guard responded. He fell trembling before Paul and Silas, and he begged them to tell him how to be saved. And it's a safe bet the guard wasn't the only conversion that night.

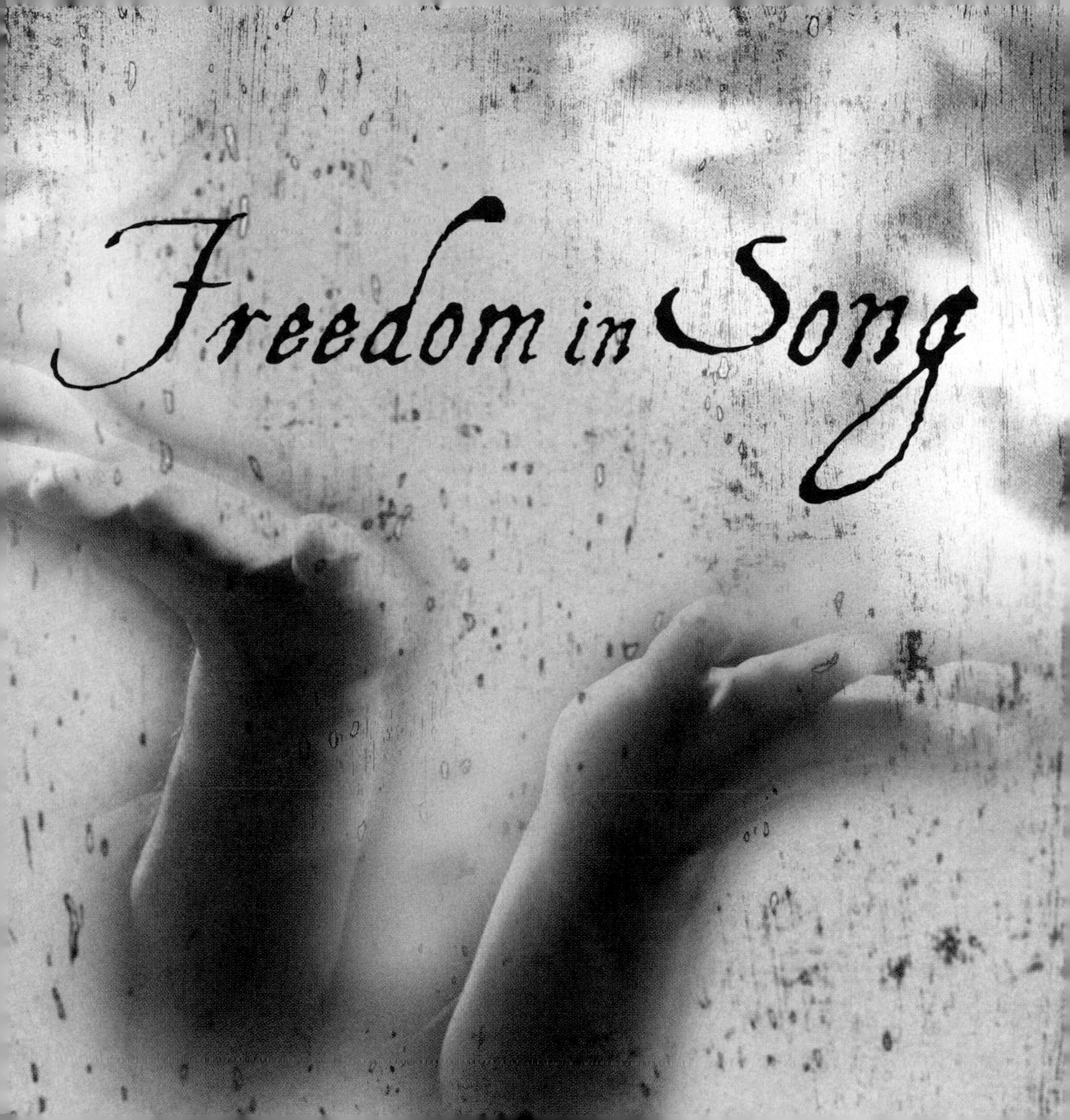
Freedom in Song

o soul, are you weary and troubled?

No light in the darkness you see?

There's a light for a look at the savior,

And life more abundant and free!

Turn your eyes upon Jesus,

Look full in His wonderful face,

And the things of earth will grow strangely dim

In the light of His glory and grace.

from the hymn "Turn Your Eyes Upon Jesus"

Helen H. Lemmel (1922)

Is anyone among you suffering?
Let him pray.
Is anyone cheerful?
Let him sing psalms.

James 5:13

All people that on earth do dwell,

　　sing to the Lord with cheerful voice;

Him serve with fear, His praise forthtell;

　　come ye before Him and rejoice.

from the hymn

"All people that on earth do dwell"

william kethe (1561)

C.S. Lewis once said that all churches should be roofless, for this very reason: worshipers would be overcome by the world God has fashioned rather than shut up in their man-made boxes.

Learn to open your eyes to the little things, to the tiny glimmers of God's presence. A couple of years ago, I was driving around and passed some Bradford pear trees in full bloom. It's hard to describe what happened next, but it was truly a spiritual experience. Something about the beauty of one of those white trees in full bloom revealed just a glimmer of God's glory, and I lost it. I had to pull over and take it all in. God was so real to me, literally pouring Himself out through the sight of that Bradford tree.

Let my lips burst forth with praise,

    for you have taught me your principles.

Let my tongue sing about your word,

    for all your commands are right.

stand ready to help me,

    for I have chosen to follow your commandments.

O Lord, I have longed for your salvation,

    and your law is my delight.

Let me live so I can praise you,

    and may your laws sustain me.

psalm 119:171-175 NLT

Worship

sustains us.

Our spirits need worship like our bodies need food.

I will sing my Maker's praises
And in Him most joyful be
For in all things I see traces
Of His tender love to me.

from the hymn
"I will sing my Maker's praises"
Paul Gerhardt (1659)

Now after Jesus was born in Bethlehem of Judea in the days of Herod the king, behold, wise men from the East came to Jerusalem, saying, "Where is He who has been born King of the Jews? For we have seen His star in the East and have come to worship Him."

MATTHEW 2:1-2

worship _is not a spectator sport._

Many times during a concert, I'll become aware that something far more profound than a performance is going on. Sitting alone at the piano, I'll be singing a song like "Thy Word," and an incredible sense of worship will settle over the arena. At that moment, I realize that I am no longer the performer. I've joined with the audience, and together we are in awe of His presence.

A Foretaste of Forever

Sing to God, not with the voice, but with the heart.

JEROME (347–420)

Then, as He was now drawing near the descent of the Mount of Olives, the whole multitude of the disciples began to rejoice and praise God with a loud voice for all the mighty works they had seen, saying:

" 'Blessed is the King who comes in the name of the LORD!' Peace in heaven and glory in the highest!"

And some of the Pharisees called to Him from the crowd, "Teacher, rebuke Your disciples."

But He answered and said to them, "I tell you that if these should keep silent, the stones would immediately cry out."

LUKE 19:37-40

Worship, done right, is a powerful thing. I've even seen people healed. The first time it ever happened to me was during a Franklin Graham festival in Spartanburg, South Carolina. We'd just finished recording the *Worship* album and it was the first time I'd ever done a whole evening of worship at a crusade. Well, we were leading worship when a man who was blind got his sight back in the middle of the worship service! I didn't know anything about it until the next day, but I believe when you have that many people who corporately worship in spirit and in truth, God shows up and things happen.

Worship

is a lifelong process.

"But the hour is coming, and now is, when the true worshipers will worship the Father in spirit and truth; for the Father is seeking such to worship Him. "God is spirit, and those who worship Him must worship in spirit and truth."

John 4:23-24

A Legacy of Worship

I it is freeing when you begin to realize it's not all about you. It's really about Him. As your children become teenagers, life seems to take on a really different meaning and your perspective changes. You start to find out what's really important in life. I've been successful and there have been a lot of great times, but I'm now faced with the question, "What lasting impression am I making on society? What are people going to remember me for?"

I want my life to be significant. For me what's significant is the kind of role model I am to my kids and to the rest of the world. Whether we realize it or not, people are watching us. All of us are role models. I was always told in Sunday school that actions speak louder than words, and as a parent that truth has hit home. You can talk all day long, but what really captures their attention is what you do. I know my kids watch what I do ten times more than they listen to what I say.

As a family, we don't sit around the piano all the time singing worship songs—although there's a part of me that wishes we did—but we try to model a lifestyle of worship in how we treat people and how we act.

We all worship—it's just a matter of who or what. Some people have "exchanged the truth of God for the lie, and worshiped and served the creature rather than the Creator" (ROMANS 1:25). But as Jesus told the Samaritan woman, "The hour is coming, and now is, when the true worshipers will worship the Father in spirit and truth; for the Father is seeking such to worship Him" (JOHN 4:23).

Worship God—in your life, in your work, in your family, in your church, in your attitude, in your friendships, in your dreams. Just worship Him.

When Michael W. Smith and a choir of other prominent Christian artists came together to record *Worship,* a live praise and worship album, fans eagerly anticipated its release—scheduled for September 11, 2001, the day terrorists struck the United States. "God's timing is always perfect," said Dean Diehl of Reunion Records. "We had no idea, obviously, that *Worship* would release on a day when people needed to hear songs like 'Draw Me Close,' 'Above All,' and 'Turn Your Eyes Upon Jesus.' *Worship* is a cry out to God for His presence, His direction and His peace."

Also from Reunion Records is *Freedom* (2000), an album of instrumentals written and produced by Michael W. Smith.

Michael W. Smith offers a patriotic look at the faith and strength of Americans in *The Price of Freedom,* a new book coming from J. Countryman® in April 2002.